Psychology Classics

Heredity, Environment, and The Question "How?"

ANNE ANASTASI

ISBN-10: 1490916660

ISBN-13: 978-1490916668

CONTENTS

A WORD FROM THE EDITOR

Originally presented by Anne Anastasi as an address of the President of the American Psychological Association in 1957 this child psychology and nature nurture debate classic argues that the question "How?" offers a much more constructive approach to the heredity-environment problem; as opposed to the question "Which one?" or "How much?"

Note To Psychology Students

If you ever have to do a paper, assignment or class project on the nature nurture debate having access to Heredity, Environment, and The Question "How?" in full will prove invaluable. A psychology classic is by definition a must read; however, most landmark texts within the discipline remain unread by a majority of psychology students. A detailed, well written description of a classic study is fine to a point, but there is absolutely no substitute for understanding and engaging with the issues under review than by reading the authors unabridged ideas, thoughts and findings in their entirety.

As a psychology student I achieved my best grades when I was able to draw upon relevant research articles in full. When establishing your position or structuring your arguments you simply have more opportunities to reflect and pick out salient points. Being able to read a classic article in full also allows you to pick out more subtle details and issues that can be overlooked. Speaking as somebody who has graded numerous papers submitted by students on the same topic, I can tell you that these more discerning observations stand out like a beacon in the dark!

Bonus Material

Heredity, Environment, and The Question "How?" builds upon some of Anne Anastasi's previously published work. Among the most notable of these earlier publications is A Proposed

Reorientation in the Heredity Environment Controversy; which is also presented in full.

About The Editor

David Webb has a first class honors degree in psychology and a Masters in Occupational psychology. For a number of years, he was a lecturer in psychology at the University of Huddersfield (UK).

He is the writer and host of four websites built around his teaching and research interests. Together these websites receive over 120,000 unique visitors each month and generate over 4 million yearly page views.

www.all-about-psychology.com

www.all-about-forensic-psychology.com

www.all-about-forensic-science.com

www.all-about-body-language.com

An active promoter of psychology through social media his psychology facebook page (www.facebook.com/psychologyonline) has over 80,000 followers and he is listed by The British Psychological Society among the top psychologists who tweet (@psych101.)

His most recent publication, The Incredibly Interesting Psychology Book (www.amazon.com/dp/B00CR1DX22) is an international #1 Best Seller.

1. A PROPOSED REORIENTATION IN THE HEREDITY ENVIRONMENT CONTROVERSY

(Anne Anastasi & John P. Foley 1948)

As more extensive and effective research procedures are brought to bear upon what has traditionally been termed the 'heredity-environment problem,' it becomes increasingly difficult for the psychologist to evade the issue on the grounds of inadequate data. The frequently repeated assertion that the crucial heredity-environment experiment has yet to be done is undoubtedly true, a fact which results in large part from difficulties in the control of experimental variables. But one wonders to what extent vague and unwieldy concepts may not have hampered the designing of definitive experiments in this area. We may be approaching a stage at which superficial methodological refinements and the accumulation of data are outstripping conceptual clarification.

When the psychologist is asked to define heredity, especially as it applies to the domain of behavior phenomena, the reply is frequently indirect, vague, or inconsistent. Nor are biologists always clear or consistent in their definitions. Thus McClung, for example, after a survey of the definitions of heredity given by various biologists, concluded that heredity has been variously conceived as a 'relation, act, fact, process, property, material, organization, rule, resemblance, or link.' It would not be difficult to add to this list on the basis of psychological writings. The concept of heredity as a 'contributing influence' and as 'potentiality' would be two obvious additions.

The diversity of views presented by psychological writers in the area of heredity and environment may be analyzed in terms of a number of 'dimensions,' or specific respects in which they differ. These differences will be considered under the rubrics of: (1) the heredity-environment relationship, (2) the nature of heredity, and (3) the nature of environment. Against this background, the traditional 'heredity-environment problem' will be re-analyzed from a logical and operational viewpoint.

THE NATURE OF THE HEREDITY ENVIRONMENT RELATIONSHIP

The interrelationship of hereditary and environmental influences in the determination of behavior has been envisaged in at least three major ways by different writers.

Isolated operation. The early classification of behavior into 'instincts' and 'habits,' corresponding to 'native behavior' and 'acquired behavior,' respectively, assumed the isolated operation of heredity and environment. Such a theory, implying the hereditary transmission of certain behavior functions in toto, has been quite generally superseded in contemporary psychology. - A comprehensive exposition of the arguments against this early 'instinct' view can be found in an article by Carmichael, appearing in 1925 (3). Although now generally admitted to be untenable, however, this belief that psychological traits can be separated into those which are acquired and those which are inherited is implied in a number of loosely expressed generalizations about the inheritance of behavior characteristics. Discussions regarding the inheritance of special talents or of such behavior patterns as 'hoarding' or 'collecting,' for example, frequently leave one with the impression that the inheritance of particular behavior traits as such was implied. Nor are more recent and more sophisticated psychological writings entirely free of such implications.

Independent additive contribution. A second possible way of conceiving the relationship between heredity and environment is in terms of a joint but independent contribution of an additive nature. According to this view, both heredity and environment contribute to all behavior development, the resulting behavior characteristics being analyzable into the sum of hereditary and environmental influences. That heredity and environment contribute jointly to behavior development is perhaps the most widely held of all views, but the additive assumption has been rarely made explicit. It should be noted, however, that this very assumption underlies all the recent attempts to determine the 'proportional contribution' of heredity and environment to the development of various behavior characteristics. The recent literature offers many estimated percentages purporting to show the degree to which intelligence test scores or some other index of performance depend upon heredity and upon environment, - especially Loevinger's detailed analysis of the 'proportional contribution' studies (11).

Interaction. The most widely recognized modus operandi of heredity and environment is that of interaction. According to this view, hereditary and environmental influences, however conceived, are regarded as mutually interacting factors in all behavior, the nature and extent of the influence of each type of factor depending upon the contribution of the other. Loevinger (11) has recently demonstrated the inconsistency of interaction with the additive assumption which underlies attempts to determine the proportional contribution of heredity and environment. Similarly, a number of years ago, Schwesinger (13) argued that the relative contribution of heredity and environment is specific not only to the trait, but also to the individual and the particular environment, i.e., under different conditions of environment, the relative contribution of heredity will differ; and under different conditions of heredity, the relative contribution of environment will differ. Haldane (6) illustrates this point very dramatically when he writes that the principal cause of illiteracy among adults under forty in modern England is either mental defect or blindness; while in modern India, lack of educational opportunity is the principal cause. Thus in the former situation, educational history accounts for a very small percentage of the variance in literacy, in the latter, it accounts for a very large percentage. It is clear that any estimate of the relative contribution of hereditary and environmental factors to individual differences depends upon the range or extent of both hereditary and environmental differences within the population under consideration. But this is by no means the only sense in which the roles of heredity and environment are mutually interdependent. The nature and extent of the influence exerted by each type of factor depend upon the contribution of the other. In other words, any one hereditary factor would operate differently under different environmental conditions. Conversely, any environmental factor would exert a different influence depending upon the specific hereditary material upon which it operates. This is essentially what is implied by Woodworth's statement (17) that the same 'objective environment' may represent different 'effective environments' for individuals of varying heredity. Varying conditions of heredity lead one individual to 'select' in a given environment different influences from those 'selected' by another individual, and in different degrees. An obvious example is the effect of a radio program upon a congenitally deaf and upon a hearing child. *Of course, each individual's previous environment, as manifested through his reactional biography, likewise determines the 'selection' of influences in the present environment. This is the point made by Kantor (10, Ch. I, II, III) when he states that objects acquire specific 'stimulus functions' through the organism's contacts with them. Thus the individual's reactional biography determines the stimulus function of any part of the environment, i.e., whether or not the object will serve as a stimulus at all and the kind of reaction which it will call forth.*

Let us consider an hypothetical illustration involving intelligence test scores. Suppose we find a 10-point difference in IQ between two identical twins reared in separate foster homes, and a 30-point difference in IQ between two unrelated children reared in the same two foster homes as the twins. Can we argue that the 10-point difference between the identical twins measures the 'differentiating effect' of these two home environments, and can we therefore analyze the 30-point difference between the unrelated children into 10 points attributable to environment and 20 points attributable to heredity? Could we conclude that, insofar as these cases show, heredity was twice as important as environment in the production of individual differences in IQ? If we follow the concept of interaction, the answer to both questions is 'No.' Actually, a very slight hereditary difference between the two unrelated children may have greatly augmented the difference between the effective environments of the two foster homes i.e., between the active stimulus value of the environments of the two unrelated children. The effective environmental difference between the two homes would thus have been much greater for the unrelated children than for the identical twins. No simple subtraction of the end-products could disentangle the relative contribution of the factors whose initial interaction led to the obtained difference in IQ.

It should also be noted that both heredity and environment represent complex manifolds of many specific influences whose relative weights may vary widely. In the previously cited illustration regarding the causes of illiteracy, for example, 'educational history' is only one specific aspect of environment, and could hardly be regarded as synonymous with it. In the same illustration, 'mental defect' and 'blindness' may themselves be the result of a wide variety of factors, environmental as well as hereditary. In the development of the individual, interaction occurs within as well as between the specific factors in each of the two categories. To speak of all the thousands of genes, each with its specific chemical and other properties, as though they represented a single force, operating as a unit to stimulate development in a particular direction, is highly misleading. It is even more clearly apparent that 'environment' is not an entity which can be contrasted or juxtaposed with 'heredity.'

Despite the almost universal acceptance of the interaction view of heredity and environment in contemporary psychological writings, statistical estimates of the degree to which 'heredity' and 'environment' account for the variance in one or another psychological trait continue to appear. It is interesting to note that some of the writers who have clearly argued for 'interaction' have themselves contributed some of these estimates of proportional contribution, presumably oblivious to the inconsistency of such a practice, *e.g., Woodworth's (17) estimates of the percentage contribution of inter-family and intra-family environmental differences in IQ, in contrast to his clear expression of the interaction view in the same monograph as well as elsewhere, also Burks' (2) computation of the percentage contribution of heredity and environment to IQ by means of path coefficients, despite her statement (1) that, "Environment may have different degrees of influence when the endowment for a given trait is of larger or smaller amount."*

Two other approaches to the analysis of hereditary and environmental contributions, although basically inconsistent with the interaction view, have found wide acceptance in recent years among psychologists who hold this view. One such approach is based on the assumption that we can measure the influence of heredity by keeping environment constant; and conversely, that we can measure the influence of environment by keeping heredity constant. It is doubtful whether the psychologically effective environment of two individuals can ever be kept constant. The condition of constant heredity, however, is fulfilled by identical twins, who have been eagerly sought by investigators for this purpose. Since the logic of the analysis is similar whether heredity or environment is kept constant, we may consider the comparison of identical twins as an illustration. Any observed behavior difference between such twins can undoubtedly be attributed to environment. The degree or extent of difference found in such a case, however, indicates little or nothing regarding the relative contribution of 'environment in general' to the production of 'individual differences in general,' since the observed inter-twin differences will themselves depend not only upon the specific nature of the environmental influences, but also upon the specific hereditary characteristics of the particular twins under observation. For example, a given environmental disparity might produce much smaller differences in the behavior of a pair of microcephalic identical twins than would occur if the twins had normal structural prerequisites for intellectual development. In other words, any estimate of the influence of 'environment' would be specific to the individuals and to the environments under consideration.

Another closely related approach is implied by the assertion that the influence of heredity becomes increasingly evident as environmental conditions improve and that the hereditary contribution would be at a maximum under conditions of 'optimum environment.' For example, as long as different groups of people are reared in communities which vary conspicuously in their educational opportunities, then individual differences in performance among adults in the total population are in part attributable to such environmental differences. It is argued, however, that as educational facilities improve, a point is approached at which each individual is offered as much education as he is capable of assimilating. At this point, individual differences in adult performance would be attributed primarily to hereditary factors.

Such an approach involves a number of possible pitfalls. First, it frequently carries the implication that the operation of heredity had been merely 'obscured' by the environmental differences, and that the 'true' contribution of heredity stands revealed under optimum conditions of environment. This argument is of course inconsistent with the concept of interaction between hereditary and environmental influences. Thus from observations made in such an 'optimum' environment, we could not generalize to other environments on the grounds that we had isolated the contribution of heredity.

Secondly, it would be very difficult to define 'optimum environment.' One may well ask, optimum for what? There seems to be an assumption here of a preordained type of development, in terms of which the most favorable environment can be identified. Thus an optimum environment is often described as one which offers no special handicaps, obstructions, or interference with the 'normal process of development.' This suggests predeterminism in the genes, and is reminiscent of the notion of the homunculus in the fertilized ovum, whose latent characteristics merely 'unfold' if given the opportunity.

When we attempt to define optimum environment in a more specific manner, we find no single continuum of 'effectiveness' in terms of which environment can be graded. The optimum environment would vary with the specific result to be achieved, e.g., high Stanford-Binet IQ, artistic aptitude, executive ability, originality, acquiescence, etc. If, now, we arbitrarily define optimum environment with reference to a specified objective, such as high Stanford-Binet IQ, a further difficulty is met in the differential effect of the same environment on different individuals. To take an hypothetical, oversimplified example, an individual who, because of certain hereditary biological factors, tends to be overactive might achieve his best intellectual development in an environment conducive to relaxation; for one who is underactive, the corresponding 'optimum' environment might be one conducive to excitement. Thus the optimum environment for the attainment of any given result will differ for each individual, unless it is assumed that behavior development is independent of any hereditary individual differences. If, however, the definition of optimum environment assumes the absence of such hereditary differences, one obviously cannot conclude that in such an optimum environment hereditary influences are at their maximum!

THE NATURE OF HEREDITY

If pressed for a concrete definition of heredity, many psychologists will suddenly leave the area of behavior resemblances and differences which they have been studying, and with a quick change of scene introduce the biological mechanism of the genes. The genes are thus regarded as the mechanism for the inheritance of psychological traits, by a sort of analogy with their demonstrated role in the transmission of structural characteristics. Regardless of how heredity is defined, however, all psychologists would undoubtedly agree that the genes play an important role in their concept of heredity. But the exact role will vary in different concepts. Some will maintain that heredity is 'carried' by the genes or that it is 'determined' by the genes. Others will insist that heredity is the genes, thus defining heredity as the specific material with which the individual begins life at conception, e.g., Jennings (8), Holt (7), Chein (4).

From a realistic, objective point of view, the genes obviously consist of specific chemical substances. They are not filled with 'potentialities,' 'tendencies,' 'influences,' 'determiners,' or other mystical entities. As Jennings puts it, "That which is directly inherited . . . is the set of genes, with the accompanying cytoplasm:-certain substances in certain combinations, which under certain conditions give rise to the individual, having certain later characteristics" (8, pp. 133-134). Similarly, Holt (7, p. 9) writes: "No potential character ever is 'already contained' in anything: and the notion of potentiality, wherever used, is a mark of finalistic thinking. The contents of the germ-cell are not potential characters at all, whether bodily or mental: they are actual proteins and other substances, and to call these substances 'potential' this or that is to flout the truth."

The fact that adult individuals differ from species to species, as well as within species, is undoubtedly related to the specific chemical constitution of the germ cells out of which each individual developed. In the same sense, an iron knocker differs from a brass knocker because of the difference in the original material out of which it was fashioned. But it would be pointless to insist that the original piece of iron contained the potentialities of the knocker, or that as the result of proper handling by a skilled worker (i.e., 'favorable' environment), its normal knocker potentialities were realized. It would have been equally 'normal' for the iron to become a horseshoe.

THE NATURE OF ENVIRONMENT

Psychologists have not only been frequently remiss in failing to sharpen and clarify their concept of 'heredity' as applied to behavior phenomena, but have often been equally vague in their use of the term 'environment.' Recognition of the implications of this term is of basic importance for an understanding of the heredity-environment problem.

'Stimulational' versus 'locational' role. Environment has been all too frequently envisaged as a passive place or 'locus' in which the organism's behavior is said to occur. In other words, the environment is regarded as a setting for behavior, rather than as an active stimulating agent. The former, passive sense of the term seems to be that characteristically implied by sociologists as well as by many psychologists. Actually, however, from a psychological point of view the environment consists of a myriad of specific stimuli which act upon the behaving organism. Strictly speaking, of course, the physical characteristics of the organism itself will in part determine the effectiveness of the environmental stimulation, as will the organism's previous 'experience,' conditioning, or reactional biography, e.g., Kantor's concept of stimulus function, 10, Ch. I, II, III.)

Specificity. The layman's notion of environment is usually a rather general or superficial geographical one, as illustrated by such descriptions as a city slum, a suburb, or a French village. A somewhat more discriminating, familial definition is implied in the frequent popular assertions that any differences in ability, interest, emotional adjustment, and the like between siblings in the same home must be the result of heredity, "since the environments were the same." An individual definition of environment recognizes the marked differences in personal relationships, participation in various activities, and the like, among individuals in the same home. It is apparent that from a psychological point of view, environment must be regarded as a complex of stimuli which is unique for each individual. Finally, the consideration of inter-cellular and intra cellular environment and their role in the processes of growth has further modified the concept of environment and has dispelled the notion of environment as an 'external' force in contrast to heredity operating 'from within.'

Temporal extent. Closely related to the scope and definition of environmental influences is the time of onset of such influences in the developmental cycle of the individual. The erroneous popular identification of heredity with that which is present at birth is reflected in the word 'native,' which signifies 'hereditary' but has the same root as 'natal' or 'pertaining to birth.' The experimental production of various monsters by the modification of the prenatal environment, as well as the extensive research on prenatal behavior development, has clearly disproved the belief that whatever is present at birth must be wholly the product of heredity. Through such experiments the starting point of environmental influences has been pushed back to the moment of conception. Moreover, experiments on the effects of radiation suggest that the genes themselves are susceptible to change in response to certain environmental agents acting even prior to fertilization. Thus the operation of environment appears to be co-extensive in time with that of heredity.

This brief examination of the heredity-environment problem suggests that the more precisely heredity and environment are defined and the more fully their operation is investigated, the more inextricably do they appear to be intertwined. Moreover, when heredity is stripped of mystical, intangible concepts and denned objectively in terms of specific chemical substances which constitute the genes, the connection between heredity and behavior appears extremely remote and indirect. The differentiation between heredity and environment is thus becoming not only increasingly difficult, but also of doubtful significance for the understanding of behavior. In fact, it might be argued that any attempt to abstract the relative contributions of 'heredity' and 'environment' becomes operationally meaningless owing to: (1) the enormous variety of specific hereditary and environmental influences; (2) the differences in their probable contributions to different behavior characteristics within the individual; (3) the differences in their probable contributions to behavior development in different individuals; and (4) the interacting nature of the operation of such factors.

Despite these almost insurmountable methodological obstacles, the issue which goes under the name of the heredity-environment problem is still very much alive. If evidence were needed for this statement it would be found in the 1940 Yearbook of the National Society for the Study of Education and in the protracted methodological controversy which has raged over the Iowa nursery school studies, as well as in the number of surveys and critical articles on the whole problem which have appeared during the past decade.

HEREDITARY-ENVIRONMENTAL VERSUS STRUCTURAL-FUNCTIONAL ANALYSIS

It is the thesis of this paper that most of the questions asked by psychologists regarding the etiology of behavior are not in effect concerned with heredity or environment, but rather with structural-or-functional factors. From the viewpoint of both the practical control of behavior and the stimulation of fruitful research, the real problem seems to be an analysis of the dependence of specific behavior characteristics upon structural conditions on the one hand or upon the individual's reactional biography on the other. The confusion of the 'structure-function' dichotomy with the 'heredity-environment' dichotomy probably underlies some of the sharpest disagreements in this field.

Theoretically, we may recognize four possible combinations among these categories. As applied to the etiology of behavior, Class A comprises those instances in which an inherited structural characteristic precludes the attainment of a specific type or degree of behavior development, as illustrated by intellectual defect associated with amaurotic juvenile idiocy. *This is one of the most clearly established instances of the role of hereditary structural characteristics in the development of feeblemindedness. A simple recessive factor is generally believed to be responsible*

14

for this condition. Even in this case, however, knowledge of the exact etiology is quite imperfect and the evidence regarding the hereditary factor still tentative.

Mental defect resulting from cerebral birth lesions represents an example of Class B. Class C is implied in assertions that there are specific genes or gene combinations corresponding to the condition of feeblemindedness per se. It is also implied by statements regarding the inheritance of artistic talent, mathematical aptitude, criminal tendencies, and the like. Class D can be illustrated by intellectual defect resulting from inadequate opportunity to learn, as in the frequently cited canal boat children, isolated mountaineers, and similar groups. In such cases, the deficiency is attributed to conditions in the individual's previous reactional biography.

It will be noted that the terms 'structural' and 'functional' as used throughout the present discussion actually refer to biological structure on the one hand and psychological function on the other. The latter is distinguished from biological functioning, which depends upon the specific properties of the structures and is more inexorably determined by such structures. *For a further discussion of the distinction between psychological, biological, and physical functioning, e.g., Kantor (9, Ch. I; 10, Ch. I and III).Given a certain type of digestive system and food, for example, digestion will occur.* But given normal human vocal structures and the auditory stimulus, "How are you?", the individual will not necessarily reply, "Fine, thank you." Depending upon his reactional biography, he may respond with, "Excuse, I speak no English," or he may merely stare in open-mouthed apathy, or possibly punch his interlocutor on the jaw. The structural-functional distinction as herein used is similar to the traditional usage of 'organic' and 'functional' in the classification of psychoses. In such a classification, 'organic' refers to the presence of specific structural deficiencies underlying the aberrant behavior; 'functional' denotes behavior disorders with no such structural deficiencies. The structural defect in organic psychoses may, however, be hereditary or environmental in origin. The distinction is not, therefore, one between inherited and environmental etiology.

Furthermore, the term 'functional psychosis' does not refer to improper biological functioning of any organ system. On the contrary, the term 'organic' is used to designate any defect either in structures or in their corresponding biological functions, i.e., either anatomical or physiological. In the same sense, 'structural' has been used in the present discussion to denote characteristics of bodily structures or of their intimately related biological functions.

What we have designated for brevity the 'structural-functional' dichotomy is at once theoretically more tenable and of more frequent practical significance than the heredity-environment distinction. In the treatment of individual cases, for example, it is of prime concern to know whether a behavioral abnormality results from structural factors on the one hand, or from such conditions as previous experience, inadequate schooling, or socio-economic level, on the other. The frequent use of the term 'constitutional,' which straddles Classes A and B, further illustrates the common reliance upon the structure-function classification. Those who believe that disembodied functions can be transmitted through the genes would also include Class C under the term 'constitutional.'

For the research psychologist, attempts to study the operation of heredity are likely to lead to fruitless or ambiguous experimental design. Reformulating the questions in terms of structural influences, regardless of the hereditary or environmental nature of the latter, would probably be a more heuristic approach. The geneticists could then tell us which structural characteristics have proved to be transmissible through the specific substance of the genes. This, however, is by no means synonymous with the statement that any one behavior characteristic is so transmissible.

A good illustration of the intertwining of heredity and environment in the structural factors which underlie behavior characteristics is furnished by recent research on the Rh factor in the blood. Among a certain percentage of 'undifferentiated feebleminded,' not classifiable under any of the traditional clinical categories, the Rh factor was found to be negative in the mother and positive in the child (e.g., 5; 14, Ch. IX; 15). These percentages have been reported to be significantly in excess of chance in most investigations to date. Geneticists have suggested that through the transfusion of blood which normally occurs between the mother and the embryo, the Rh incompatibility may produce a condition of insufficient oxygen; if this, in turn, occurs at a critical stage of brain development in the embryo, feeblemindedness may result. Thus, although the Rh factor is hereditary, such feeblemindedness would not be hereditary, but would be acquired by the embryo as an environmental effect. The investigator interested in determining whether 'constitutional factors' or 'opportunity to learn' were of prime importance in a particular case, however, would hardly classify the Rh factor under the latter!

A similar point may be made in reference to cerebral birth lesions. These are clearly environmental factors, but little would be gained by classing them together with socio-economic level and nursery school attendance. Furthermore, it could be argued that hereditary factors probably play a part in the development of such characteristics as cranial conformation in the child or pelvic dimensions in the mother, such conditions in turn influencing the likelihood of cerebral birth injuries. Thus with reference to behavior development, heredity may enter into the operation of such 'environmental conditions' as birth lesions, and conversely, environment may be involved in the operation of such 'hereditary influences' as the Rh factor.

It should be noted that the most common source of disagreement between 'hereditarians' and 'environmentalists' in psychology pertains to Class C, viz., 'inherited functional characteristics.' We may consider, for example, the widely quoted and much maligned statement by John B. Watson: "Give me a dozen healthy infants, well formed, and my own specified world to bring them up in and I'll guarantee to take any one at random and train him to become any

17

type of specialist I might select-doctor, lawyer, artist, merchant chief and, yes, even beggar-man and thief, regardless of his talents, penchants, tendencies, abilities, vocations, and race of his ancestors" (16, p. 104). In the light of its context, it appears very likely that this statement represented only a protest against the type of behavior etiology indicated by Class C. The statement might thus be paraphrased to read: "Given a group of children with normal structural prerequisites, any behavioral variance among them can be attributed to their respective reactional biographies." Much confusion has resulted from the failure to realize that the terms 'healthy' and 'well-formed' in Watson's statement implied freedom from any structural deficiencies that might be relevant to behavior development. *To be sure, Watson's statement seems to imply that structural characteristics must be 'pathological' in degree in order to influence behavior development. He does not appear to consider the possibility that normal variations in structural characteristics within the species may limit behavior development in particular directions.* It was the inheritance of psychological functions as such that this statement rejected.

Many allegedly 'extreme hereditarians' would probably agree that no behavior as such is inherited, and that they are merely arguing for the importance of Class A and Class E factors, as contrasted to Class D factors, in the etiology of certain specific behavior characteristics. Thus the more explicit formulation of the problem immediately reveals the superficial nature of the disagreement.

The proposed analysis of behavior etiology into structural-and-functional rather than hereditary-and-environmental factors does not imply any attempt to 'reduce' psychological functions to biological or physical ones, or to 'explain' one in terms of the other. Explanations of behavior must of course be sought among behavior phenomena themselves. It is well known that attempts to 'explain' psychological phenomena in biological terms have often produced only animistic notions in a pseudo-neurological guise. This matter has been fully discussed by Kantor, who concludes: "Not only must we not regard

18

psychological conduct as sheer biological activity, but also we cannot look upon the biological concomitants of psychological responses as the causes of the latter...Probably the most effective way is to consider the biological factors as participants in the psychological response - namely, the operations of the biological mechanisms are factors in a psychological event" (10, pp. 49-50). In so far as structural factors are 'participants,' however, their study will aid in the understanding of behavior by furnishing a more complete picture of the conditions under which specific behavior characteristics appear.

In summary, it is proposed that the etiology of behavior be approached in terms of structural contributions versus the contributions of reactional biography, rather than in terms of the traditional heredity-environment dichotomy. It has become increasingly apparent that the operation of heredity is inextricably linked with that of environment. Moreover, since heredity must necessarily operate through the medium of structural factors, it follows that the applicability of the concept of heredity to behavior phenomena is indirect and remote. In the light of these theoretical considerations, as well as from a heuristic and a practical point of view, the structural-functional analysis of behavior appears to be more productive than that in terms of heredity and environment.

REFERENCES

1. BURKS, B S Statistical hazards in nature-nurture investigations. Yearbook, Nat. Soc. Stud. Educ., 1928, 27, Part I, 9-33.

2. BURKS, B S The relative influence of nature and nurture upon mental development; a comparative study of foster parent-foster child resemblance and true parent-true child resemblance Yearbook, Nat Soc. Stud Educ, 1928, 27, Part I, 219-316.

3. CARMICHAEL, L. Heredity and environment: are they antithetical? J. abn. soc. Psychol, 1925, 20, 24S-260.

4. CHEDJ, I. The problems of heredity and environment. J. Psychol., 1936, 2, 229-244.

5. COOK, R. The Rh gene as a cause of mental deficiency. J. Hered., 1944, 35, 133-134.

6. HALDANE, J. B S. Heredity and politics. New York. Norton, 1938 Pp. 202.

7. HOLT, E. B Animal drive and the learning process. New York-Holt, 1931. Pp. 307

8. JENNINGS, H. S. The biological basis of human nature. New York: Norton, 1930. Pp 384

9. KANTOR, J. R. Principles of psychology. New York: Knopf, 1924 Vol. I, pp. 473.

10. KANTOR, J. R A survey of the science of psychology Bloomington, Ind.: Principia Press. 1933. Pp. 564.

11. LOEVINGER, J. On the proportional contributions of differences in nature and in nurture to differences in intelligence Psychol. Bull., 1943, 40, 725-756

12. MCCLUNG, C E. The heredity of sex. In Our present knowledge of heredity. Mayo Foundation Lectures, 1923-24. St. Louis- Saunders, 1925. Pp. 250

13. SCHWESINGER, G. C. Heredity and environment. New York: Macmillan, 1933. Pp 484

14. SNYDER, L H. The principles of heredity (3rd ed.) Boston: Heath, 1946. Pp. 450.

15. SNYDER, L H , SCHONFELD, M D., & OFFERMAN, E. M. A further note on the Rh factor and feeblemindedness. J. Hered., 1945, 36, 534.

16. WATSON, J B. Behaviorism. New York: Norton, 1930. Pp 308

17. WOODWORTH, R. S. Heredity and environment: a critical survey of recently published material on twins and foster children. Soc. Sci. Res. Council Bull., 1941, No. 47. Pp. 96.

2. HEREDITY, ENVIRONMENT, AND THE QUESTION "HOW?"

(Anne Anastasi 1958)

Two or three decades ago, the so called heredity-environment question was the center of lively controversy. Today, on the other hand, many psychologists look upon it as a dead issue. It is now generally conceded that both hereditary and environmental factors enter into all behavior. The reacting organism is a product of its genes and its past environment, while present environment provides the immediate stimulus for current behavior. To be sure, it can be argued that, although a given trait may result from the combined influence of hereditary and environmental factors, a specific difference in this trait between individuals or between groups may be traceable to either hereditary or environmental factors alone. The design of most traditional investigations undertaken to identify such factors, however, has been such as to yield inconclusive answers. The same set of data has frequently led to opposite conclusions in the hands of psychologists with different orientations.

Nor have efforts to determine the proportional contribution of hereditary and environmental factors to observed individual differences in given traits met with any greater success. Apart from difficulties in controlling conditions, such investigations have usually been based upon the implicit assumption that hereditary and environmental factors combine in an additive fashion. Both geneticists and psychologists have repeatedly demonstrated, however, that a more tenable hypothesis is that of interaction (15, 22, 28, 40). In other words, the nature and extent of the influence of each type of factor depend upon the contribution of the other. Thus the proportional contribution of heredity to the variance of a given trait, rather than being a constant, will vary under different environmental conditions. Similarly, under different hereditary conditions, the relative contribution of environment will differ. Studies designed to estimate the proportional contribution of heredity and environment, however, have rarely included measures of such interaction. The only possible conclusion from such research would thus seem to be that both heredity and environment contribute to all behavior traits and that the extent of their respective contributions cannot be specified for any trait. Small wonder that some psychologists regard the heredity environment question as unworthy of further consideration!

But is this really all we can find out about the operation of heredity and environment in the etiology of behavior? Perhaps we have simply been asking the wrong questions. The traditional questions about heredity and environment may be intrinsically unanswerable. Psychologists began by asking which type of factor, hereditary or environmental, is responsible for individual differences in a given trait. Later, they tried to discover how much of the variance was attributable to heredity and how much to environment. It is the primary contention of this paper that a more fruitful approach is to be found in the question "How?" There is still much to be learned about the specific modus operandi of hereditary and environmental factors in the development of behavioral differences. And there are several current lines of research which offer promising techniques for answering the question "How?"

VARIETY OF INTERACTION MECHANISMS

Hereditary Factors

If we examine some of the specific ways in which hereditary factors may influence behavior, we cannot fail but be impressed by their wide diversity. At one extreme, we find such conditions as phenylpyruvic amentia and amaurotic idiocy. In these cases, certain essential physical prerequisites for normal intellectual development are lacking as a result of hereditary metabolic disorders. In our present state of knowledge, there is no environmental factor which can completely counteract this hereditary deficit. The individual will be mentally defective, regardless of the type of environmental conditions under which he is reared.

A somewhat different situation is illustrated by hereditary deafness, which may lead to intellectual retardation through interference with normal social interaction, language development, and schooling. In such a case, however, the hereditary handicap can be offset by appropriate adaptations of training procedures. It has been said, in fact, that the degree of intellectual backwardness of the deaf is an index of the state of development of special instructional facilities. As the latter improve, the intellectual retardation associated with deafness is correspondingly reduced. A third example is provided by inherited susceptibility to certain physical diseases, with consequent protracted ill health. If environmental conditions are such that illness does in fact develop, a number of different behavioral effects may follow. Intellectually, the individual may be handicapped by his inability to attend school regularly. On the other hand, depending upon age of onset, home conditions, parental status, and similar factors, poor health may have the effect of concentrating the individual's energies upon intellectual pursuits. The curtailment of participation in athletics and social functions may serve to strengthen interest in reading and other sedentary activities. Concomitant circumstances would also determine the influence of such illness upon personality development. And it is well known that the latter effects could run the gamut from a deepening of human sympathy to psychiatric breakdown.

Finally, heredity may influence behavior through the mechanism of social stereotypes. A wide variety of inherited physical characteristics have served as the visible cues for identifying such stereotypes. These cues thus lead to behavioral restrictions or opportunities and-at a more subtle level -to social attitudes and expectancies. The individual's own self concept tends gradually to reflect such expectancies. All of these influences eventually leave their mark upon his abilities and inabilities, his emotional reactions, goals, ambitions, and outlook on life.

The geneticist Dobzhansky illustrates this type of mechanism by means of a dramatic hypothetical situation. He points out that, if there were a culture in which the carriers of blood group AB were considered aristocrats and those of blood group O laborers, then the blood group genes would become important hereditary determiners of behavior (12, p. 147). Obviously the association between blood group and behavior would be specific to that culture. But such specificity is an essential property of the causal mechanism under consideration. More realistic examples are not hard to find. The most familiar instances occur in connection with constitutional types, sex, and race. Sex and skin pigmentation obviously depend upon heredity. General body build is strongly influenced by hereditary components, although also susceptible to environmental modification. That all these physical characteristics may exert a pronounced effect upon behavior within a given culture is well known. It is equally apparent, of course, that in different cultures the behavioral correlates of such hereditary physical traits may be quite unlike. A specific physical cue may be completely unrelated to individual differences in psychological traits in one culture, while closely correlated with them in another. Or it may be associated with totally dissimilar behavior characteristics in two different cultures.

It might be objected that some of the illustrations which have been cited do not properly exemplify the operation of hereditary mechanisms in behavior development, since hereditary factors enter only indirectly into the behavior in question. Closer examination, however, shows this distinction to be untenable. First it may be noted that the influence of heredity upon behavior is always indirect. No psychological trait is ever inherited as such. All we can ever say directly from behavioral observations is that a given trait shows evidence of being influenced by certain "inheritable unknowns." This merely defines a problem for genetic research; it does not provide a causal explanation. Unlike the blood groups, which are close to the level of primary gene products, psychological traits are related to genes by highly indirect and devious routes. Even the mental deficiency associated with phenylketonuria is several steps removed from the chemically defective genes that represent its hereditary basis. Moreover, hereditary influences cannot be dichotomized into the more direct and the less direct. Rather do they represent a whole "continuum of indirectness," along which are found all degrees of remoteness of causal links. The examples already cited illustrate a few of the points on this continuum.

It should be noted that as we proceed along the continuum of indirectness, the range of variation of possible outcomes of hereditary factors expands rapidly. At each step in the causal chain, there is fresh opportunity for interaction with other hereditary factors as well as with environmental factors. And since each interaction in turn determines the direction of subsequent interactions, there is an ever-widening network of possible outcomes. If we visualize a simple sequential grid with only two alternatives at each point, it is obvious that there are two possible outcomes in the one-stage situation, four outcomes at the second stage, eight at the third, and so on in geometric progression. The actual situation is undoubtedly much more complex, since there will usually be more than two alternatives at any one point.

In the case of the blood groups, the relation to specific genes is so close that no other concomitant hereditary or environmental conditions can alter the outcome. If the organism survives at all, it will have the blood group determined by its genes. Among psychological traits, on the other hand, some variation in outcome is always possible as a result of concurrent circumstances. Even in cases of phenylketonuria, intellectual development will exhibit some relationship with the type of care and training available to the individual. That behavioral outcomes show progressive diversification as we proceed along the continuum of indirectness is brought out by the other examples which were cited. Chronic illness can lead to scholarly renown or to intellectual immaturity; a mesomorphic physique can be a contributing factor in juvenile delinquency or in the attainment of a college presidency! Published data on Sheldon somatotypes provide some support for both of the latter outcomes.

Parenthetically, it may be noted that geneticists have sometimes used the term "norm of reaction" to designate the range of variation of possible outcomes of gene properties (cf. 13, p. 161). Thus heredity sets the "norm" or limits within which environmental differences determine the eventual outcome. In the case of some traits, such as blood groups or eye color, this norm is much narrower than in the case of other traits. Owing to the rather different psychological connotations of both the words "norm" and "reaction," however, it seems less confusing to speak of the "range of variation" in this context.

A large portion of the continuum of hereditary influences which we have described coincides with the domain of somatopsychological relations, as denned by Barker et al. (6). Under this heading, Barker includes "variations in physique that affect the psychological situation of a person by influencing the effectiveness of his body as a tool for actions or by serving as a stimulus to himself or others" (6, p.1). Relatively direct neurological influences on behavior, which have been the traditional concern of physiological psychology, are excluded from this definition, Barker being primarily concerned with what he calls the "social psychology of physique." Of the examples cited in the present paper, deafness, severe illness, and the physical characteristics associated with social stereotypes would meet the specifications of somatopsychological factors.

The somatic factors to which Barker refers, however, are not limited to those of hereditary origin. Bodily conditions attributable to environmental causes operate in the same sorts of somatopsychological relations as those traceable to heredity. In fact, heredity-environment distinctions play a minor part in Barker's approach.

Environmental Factors: Organic

Turning now to an analysis of the role of environmental factors in behavior, we find the same etiological mechanisms which were observed in the case of hereditary factors. First, however, we must differentiate between two classes of environmental influences: (a) those producing organic effects which may in turn influence behavior and (b) those serving as direct stimuli for psychological reactions. The former may be illustrated by food intake or by exposure to bacterial infection; the latter, by tribal initiation ceremonies or by a course in algebra. There are no completely satisfactory names by which to designate these two classes of influences. In an earlier paper by Anastasi and Foley (4), the terms "structural" and "functional" were employed. However, "organic" and "behavioral" have the advantage of greater familiarity in this context and may be less open to misinterpretation. Accordingly, these terms will be used in the present paper.

Like hereditary factors, environmental influences of an organic nature can also be ordered along a continuum of indirectness with regard to their relation to behavior. This continuum closely parallels that of hereditary factors. One end is typified by such conditions as mental deficiency resulting from cerebral birth injury or from prenatal nutritional inadequacies. A more indirect etiological mechanism is illustrated by severe motor disorder-as in certain cases of cerebral palsy-without accompanying injury to higher neurological centers. In such instances, intellectual retardation may occur as an indirect result of the motor handicap, through the curtailment of educational and social activities. Obviously this causal mechanism corresponds closely to that of hereditary deafness cited earlier in the paper.

Finally, we may consider an environmental parallel to the previously discussed social stereotypes which were mediated by hereditary physical cues. Let us suppose that a young woman with mousy brown hair becomes transformed into a dazzling golden blonde through environmental techniques currently available in our culture. It is highly probable that this metamorphosis will alter, not only the reactions of her associates toward her, but also her own self concept and subsequent behavior. The effects could range all the way from a rise in social poise to a drop in clerical accuracy!

Among the examples of environmentally determined organic influences which have been described, all but the first two fit Barker's definition of somatopsychological factors. With the exception of birth injuries and nutritional deficiencies, all fall within the social psychology of physique. Nevertheless, the individual factors exhibit wide diversity in their specific modus operandi - a diversity which has important practical as well as theoretical implications.

Environmental Factors: Behavioral

The second major class of environmental factors-the behavioral as contrasted to the organic-are by definition direct influences. The immediate effect of such environmental factors is always a behavioral change. To be sure, some of the initial behavioral effects may themselves indirectly affect the individual's later behavior. But this relationship can perhaps be best conceptualized in terms of breadth and permanence of effects. Thus it could be said that we are now dealing, not with a continuum of indirectness, as in the case of hereditary and organic-environmental factors, but rather with a continuum of breadth.

Social class membership may serve as an illustration of a relatively broad, pervasive, and enduring environmental factor. Its influence upon behavior development may operate through many channels. Thus social level may determine the range and nature of intellectual stimulation provided by home and community through books, music, art, play activities, and the like. Even more far-reaching may be the effects upon interests and motivation, as illustrated by the desire to perform abstract intellectual tasks, to surpass others in competitive situations, to succeed in school, or to gain social approval. Emotional and social traits may likewise be influenced by the nature of interpersonal relations characterizing homes at different socioeconomic levels. Somewhat more restricted in scope than social class, although still exerting a relatively broad influence, is amount of formal schooling which the individual is able to obtain.

A factor which may be wide or narrow in its effects, depending upon concomitant circumstances, is language handicap. Thus the bilingualism of an adult who moves to a foreign country with inadequate mastery of the new language represents a relatively limited handicap which can be readily overcome in most cases. At most, the difficulty is one of communication. On the other hand, some kinds of bilingualism in childhood may exert a retarding influence upon intellectual development and may under certain conditions affect personality development adversely (2, 5, 10). A common pattern in the homes of immigrants is that the child speaks one language at home and another in school, so that his knowledge of each language is limited to certain types of situations. Inadequate facility with the language of the school interferes with the acquisition of basic concepts, intellectual skills, and information. The frustration engendered by scholastic difficulties may in turn lead to discouragement and general dislike of school. Such reactions can be found, for example, among a number of Puerto Rican children in New York City schools (3). In the case of certain groups, moreover, the child's foreign language background may be perceived by himself and his associates as a symbol of minority group status and may thereby augment any emotional maladjustment arising from such status (34).

A highly restricted environmental influence is to be found in the opportunity to acquire specific items of information occurring in a particular intelligence test. The fact that such opportunities may vary with culture, social class, or individual experiential background is at the basis of the test user's concern with the problem of coaching and with "culture-free" or "culture-fair" tests (cf. 1, 2). If the advantage or disadvantage which such experiential differences confer upon certain individuals is strictly confined to performance on the given test, it will obviously reduce the validity of the test and should be eliminated.

In this connection, however, it is essential to know the breadth of the environmental influence in question. A fallacy inherent in many attempts to develop culture-fair tests is that the breadth of cultural differentials is not taken into account. Failure to consider breadth of effect likewise characterizes certain discussions of coaching. If, in coaching a student for a college admission test, we can improve his knowledge of verbal concepts and his reading comprehension, he will be better equipped to succeed in college courses. His performance level will thus be raised, not only on the test, but also on the criterion which the test is intended to predict. To try to devise a test which is not susceptible to such coaching would merely reduce the effectiveness of the test. Similarly, efforts to rule out cultural differentials from test items so as to make them equally "fair" to subjects in different social classes or in different cultures may merely limit the usefulness of the test, since the same cultural differentials may operate within the broader area of behavior which the test is designed to sample.

METHODOLOGICAL APPROACHES

The examples considered so far should suffice to highlight the wide variety of ways in which hereditary and environmental factors may interact in the course of behavior development. There is clearly a need for identifying explicitly the etiological mechanism whereby any given hereditary or environmental condition ultimately leads to a behavioral characteristic-in other words, the "how" of heredity and environment. Accordingly, we may now take a quick look at some promising methodological approaches to the question "how."

Within the past decade, an increasing number of studies have been designed to trace the connection between specific factors in the hereditary backgrounds or in the reactional biographies of individuals and their observed behavioral characteristics. There has been a definite shift away from the predominantly descriptive and correlational approach of the earlier decades toward more deliberate attempts to verify explanatory hypotheses. Similarly, the cataloguing of group differences in psychological traits has been giving way gradually to research on changes in group characteristics following altered conditions.

Among recent methodological developments, we have chosen seven as being particularly relevant to the analysis of etiological mechanisms. The first represents an extension of selective breeding investigations to permit the identification of specific hereditary conditions underlying the observed behavioral differences. When early selective breeding investigations such as those of Tryon (36) on rats indicated that "maze learning ability" was inherited, we were still a long way from knowing what was actually being transmitted by the genes. It was obviously not "maze learning ability" as such. Twenty - or even ten - years ago, some psychologists would have suggested that it was probably general intelligence. And a few might even have drawn a parallel with the inheritance of human intelligence.

But today investigators have been asking: Just what makes one group of rats learn mazes more quickly than the other? Is it differences in motivation, emotionality, speed of running, general activity level? If so, are these behavioral characteristics in turn dependent upon group differences in glandular development, body weight, brain size, biochemical factors, or some other organic conditions? A number of recent and ongoing investigations indicate that attempts are being made to trace, at least part of the way, the steps whereby certain chemical properties of the genes may ultimately lead to specified behavior characteristics.

An example of such a study is provided by Searle's (31) follow-up of Tryon's research. Working with the strains of maze-bright and maze-dull rats developed by Tryon, Searle demonstrated that the two strains differed in a number of emotional and motivational factors, rather than in ability. Thus the strain differences were traced one step further, although many links still remain to be found between maze learning and genes. A promising methodological development within the same general area is to be found in the recent research of Hirsch and Tryon (18). Utilizing a specially devised technique for measuring individual differences in behavior among lower organisms, these investigators launched a series of studies on selective breeding for behavioral characteristics in the fruit fly, Drosophila. Such research can capitalize on the mass of available genetic knowledge regarding the morphology of Drosophila, as well as on other advantages of using such an organism in genetic studies.

Further evidence of current interest in the specific hereditary factors which influence behavior is to be found in an extensive research program in progress at the Jackson Memorial Laboratory, under the direction of Scott and Fuller (30). In general, the project is concerned with the behavioral characteristics of various breeds and cross-breeds of dogs. Analyses of some of the data gathered to date again suggest that "differences in performance are produced by differences in emotional, motivational, and peripheral processes, and that genetically caused differences in central processes may be either slight or non-existent" (29, p. 225). In other parts of the same project, breed differences in physiological characteristics, which may in turn be related to behavioral differences, have been established.

A second line of attack is the exploration of possible relationships between behavioral characteristics and physiological variables which may in turn be traceable to hereditary factors. Research on EEC, autonomic balance, metabolic processes, and biochemical factors illustrates this approach. A lucid demonstration of the process of tracing a psychological condition to genetic factors is provided by the identification and subsequent investigation of phenylpyruvic amentia. In this case, the causal chain from defective gene, through metabolic disorder and consequent cerebral malfunctioning, to feeblemindedness and other overt symptoms can be described step by step (cf. 32; 33, pp. 389-391). Also relevant are the recent researches on neurological and biochemical correlates of schizophrenia (9). Owing to inadequate methodological controls, however, most of the findings of the latter studies must be regarded as tentative (19).

Prenatal environmental factors provide a third avenue of fruitful investigation. Especially noteworthy is the recent work of Pasamanick and his associates (27), which demonstrated a tie-up between socioeconomic level, complications of pregnancy and parturition, and psychological disorders of the offspring. In a series of studies on large samples of whites and Negroes in Baltimore, these investigators showed that various prenatal and paranatal disorders are significantly related to the occurrence of mental defect and psychiatric disorders in the child. An important source of such irregularities in the process of childbearing and birth is to be found in deficiencies of maternal diet and in other conditions associated with low socioeconomic status. An analysis of the data did in fact reveal a much higher frequency of all such medical complications in lower than in higher socioeconomic levels, and a higher frequency among Negroes than among whites.

Direct evidence of the influence of prenatal nutritional factors upon subsequent intellectual development is to be found in a recent, well controlled experiment by Harrell et al. (16). The subjects were pregnant women in low income groups, whose normal diets were generally quite deficient. A dietary supplement was administered to some of these women during pregnancy and lactation, while an equated control group received placebos. When tested at the ages of three and four years, the offspring of the experimental group obtained a significantly higher mean IQ than did the offspring of the controls.

Mention should also be made of animal experiments on the effects of such factors as prenatal radiation and neonatal asphyxia upon cerebral anomalies as well as upon subsequent behavior development. These experimental studies merge imperceptibly into the fourth approach to be considered, namely, the investigation of the influence of early experience upon the eventual behavioral characteristics of animals. Research in this area has been accumulating at a rapid rate. In 19 54, Beach and Jaynes (8) surveyed this literature for the Psychological Bulletin, listing over 130 references. Several new studies have appeared since that date (e.g., 14, 21, 24, 25, 35). The variety of factors covered ranges from the type and quantity of available food to the extent of contact with human culture. A large number of experiments have been concerned with various forms of sensory deprivation and with diminished opportunities for motor exercise. Effects have been observed in many kinds of animals and in almost all aspects of behavior, including perceptual responses, motor activity, learning, emotionality, and social reactions

In their review, Beach and Jaynes pointed out that research in this area has been stimulated by at least four distinct theoretical interests. Some studies were motivated by the traditional concern with the relative contribution of maturation and learning to behavior development. Others were designed in an effort to test certain psychoanalytic theories regarding infantile experiences, as illustrated by studies which limited the feeding responses of young animals. A third relevant influence is to be found in the work of the European biologist Lorenz (23) on early social stimulation of birds, and in particular on the special type of learning for which the term "imprinting" has been coined. A relatively large number of recent studies have centered around Hebb's (17) theory regarding the importance of early perceptual experiences upon subsequent performance in learning situations. All this research represents a rapidly growing and promising attack on the modus operandi of specific environmental factors.

The human counterpart of these animal studies may be found in the comparative investigation of child-rearing practices in different cultures and subcultures. This represents the fifth approach in our list. An outstanding example of such a study is that by Whiting and Child (38), published in 1953. Utilizing data on 75 primitive societies from the Cross-Cultural Files of the Yale Institute of Human Relations, these investigators set out to test a number of hypotheses regarding the relationships between child-rearing practices and personality development. This analysis was followed up by field observations in five cultures, the results of which have not yet been reported (cf. 37).

Within our own culture, similar surveys have been concerned with the diverse psychological environments provided by different social classes (11). Of particular interest are the study by Williams and Scott (39) on the association between socioeconomic level, permissiveness, and motor development among Negro children, and the exploratory research by Milner (26) on the relationship between reading readiness in first-grade children and patterns of parent-child interaction. Milner found that upon school entrance the lowerclass child seems to lack chiefly two advantages enjoyed by the middle-class child. The first is described as "a warm positive family atmosphere or adult-relationship pattern which is more and more being recognized as a motivational prerequisite of any kind of adult-controlled learning." The lower-class children in Milner's study perceived adults as predominantly hostile. The second advantage is an extensive opportunity to interact verbally with adults in the family. The latter point is illustrated by parental attitudes toward mealtime conversation, lower-class parents tending to inhibit and discourage such conversation, while middle-class parents encourage it.

Most traditional studies on child-rearing practices have been designed in terms of a psychoanalytic orientation. There is need for more data

36

pertaining to other types of hypotheses. Findings such as those of Milner on opportunities for verbalization and the resulting effects upon reading readiness represent a step in this direction. Another possible source of future data is the application of the intensive observational techniques of psychological ecology developed by Barker and Wright (7) to widely diverse socioeconomic groups.

A sixth major approach involves research on the previously cited somatopsychological relationships (6). To date, little direct information is available on the precise operation of this class of factors in psychological development. The multiplicity of ways in which physical traits-whether hereditary or environmental in origin-may influence behavior thus offers a relatively unexplored field for future study.

The seventh and final approach to be considered represents an adaptation of traditional twin studies. From the standpoint of the question "How?" there is need for closer coordination between the usual data on twin resemblance and observations of the family interactions of twins. Available data already suggest, for example, that closeness of contact and extent of environmental similarity are greater in the case of monozygotic than in the case of dizygotic twins (cf. 2). Information on the social reactions of twins toward each other and the specialization of roles is likewise of interest (2). Especially useful would be longitudinal studies of twins, beginning in early infancy and following the subjects through school age. The operation of differential environmental pressures, the development of specialized roles, and other environmental influences could thus be more clearly identified and correlated with intellectual and personality changes in the growing twins.

Parenthetically, I should like to add a remark about the traditional applications of the twin method, in which persons in different degrees of hereditary and environmental relationships to each other are simply compared for behavioral similarity. In these studies, attention has been focused principally upon the amount of resemblance of monozygotic as contrasted to dizygotic twins. Yet such a comparison is particularly difficult to interpret because of the many subtle differences in the environmental situations of the two types of twins. A more fruitful comparison would seem to be that between dizygotic twins and siblings, for whom the hereditary similarity is known to be the same. In Kallmann's monumental research on psychiatric disorders among twins (20), for example, one of the most convincing bits of evidence for the operation of hereditary factors in schizophrenia is the fact that the degrees of concordance for dizygotic twins and for siblings were practically identical. In contrast, it will be recalled that in intelligence test scores dizygotic twins resemble each other much more closely than do siblings-a finding which reveals the influence of environmental factors in intellectual development.

SUMMARY

The heredity-environment problem is still very much alive. Its viability is assured by the gradual replacement of the questions, "Which one?" and "How much?" by the more basic and appropriate question, "How?" Hereditary influences- as well as environmental factors of an organic nature-vary along a "continuum of indirectness." The more indirect their connection with behavior, the wider will be the range of variation of possible outcomes. One extreme of the continuum of indirectness may be illustrated by brain damage leading to mental deficiency; the other extreme, by physical characteristics associated with social stereotypes. Examples of factors falling at intermediate points include deafness, physical diseases, and motor disorders. Those environmental factors which act directly upon behavior can be ordered along a continuum of breadth or permanence of effect, as exemplified by social class membership, amount of formal schooling, language handicap, and familiarity with specific test items.

Several current lines of research offer promising techniques for exploring the modus operandi of hereditary and environmental factors. Outstanding among them are investigations of: (a) hereditary conditions which underlie behavioral differences between selectively bred groups of animals; (b) relations between physiological variables and individual differences in behavior, especially in the case of pathological deviations; (c) role of prenatal physiological factors in behavior development; (d) influence of early experience upon eventual behavioral characteristics; (e) cultural differences in child-rearing practices in relation to intellectual and emotional development; (f) mechanisms of somatopsychological relationships; and (g) psychological development of twins from infancy to maturity, together with observations of their social environment. Such approaches are extremely varied with regard to subjects employed, nature of psychological functions studied, and specific experimental procedures followed. But it is just such heterogeneity of methodology that is demanded by the wide diversity of ways in which hereditary and environmental factors interact in behavior development.

REFERENCES

1. ANASTASI, ANNE. Psychological testing. New York: Macmillan, 1954.

2. ANASTASI, ANNE. Differential psychology. (3rd ed.) New York: Macmillan, 1958.

3.ANASTASI, ANNE, & CORDOVA, F. A. Some effects of bilingualism upon the intelligence test performance of Puerto Rican children in New York City. J. educ. Psychol, 1953, 44, 1-19.

4.ANASTASI, ANNE, & FOLEY, J. P., JR. A proposed reorientation in the heredity environment controversy. Psychol. Rev., 1948, 55, 239-249.

5. ARSENIAN, S. Bilingualism in the postwar world. Psychol. Bull,

1945, 42, 65-86.

6. BARKER, R. G., WRIGHT, BEATRICE A., MYERSON, L., & GONICK, MOIXIE R. Adjustment to physical handicap and illness: A survey of the social psychology of physique and disability. Soc. Sci. Res. Coun. Bull., 1953, No. 55 (Rev.)

7. BARKER, R. G., & WRIGHT, H. F. Midwest and its children: The psychological ecology of an American town. Evanston, 111.: Row, Peterson, 1955.

8. BEACH, F. A., & JAYNES, J. Effects of early experience upon the behavior of animals. Psychol. Bull., 1954, 51, 239-263.

9. BRACKBIIX, G. A. Studies of brain dysfunction in schizophrenia. Psychol. Bull., 1956, 53, 210-226.

10. DARCY, NATALIE T. A review of the literature on the effects of bilingualism upon the measurement of intelligence. G. genet. Psychol., 1953, 82, 21-57.

11. DAVIS, A., & HAVIGHURST, R. J. Social class and color differences in child rearing. Amer. social. Rev., 1946, 11, 698-710.

12. DOBZHANSKY, T. The genetic nature of differences among men. In S. Persons (Ed.), Evolutionary thought in America. New Haven: Yale Univer. Press, 1950. Pp. 86-155.

13. DOBZHANSKY, T. Heredity, environment, and evolution. Science, 1950, 111, 161-166.

14. FORGUS, R. H. The effect of early perceptual learning on the behavioral organization of adult rats. J. comp. physiol. Psychol., 1954, 47, 331-336.

15. HALDANE, J. B. S. Heredity and politics. New York: Norton, 1938.

16. HARRELL, RUTH F., WOODYARD, ELLA, & GATES, A. I. The effect of mothers' diets on the intelligence of the offspring. New York: Bur. Publ., Teach. Coll., Columbia Univer., 1955.

17. HEBB, D. O. The organization of behavior. New York: Wiley, 1949.

18. HIRSCH, J., & TRYON, R. C. Mass screening and reliable individual measurement in the experimental behavior genetics of lower organisms. Psychol. Bull., 1956, 53, 402-410.

19. HORWITT, M. K. Fact and artifact in the biology of schizophrenia. Science, 1956, 124, 429-430.

20.KALLMANN, F. J. Heredity in health and mental disorder; Principles of psychiatric genetics in the light of comparative twin studies. New York: Norton, 1953.

21. KING, J. A., & GURNEY, NANCY L. Effect of early social experience on adult aggressive behavior in C57BL10 mice. J. comp. physiol. Psychol., 1954, 47, 326-330.

22. LOEVINGER, JANE. On the proportional contributions of differences in nature and in nurture to differences in intelligence. Psychol. Bull., 1943, 40, 725-756.

23. LORENZ, K. Der Kumpan in der Unwell des Vogels. Der Artgenosse als aus-16'sendes Moment sozialer Verhaltungsweisen. J. Orn., Lpz., 1935, 83, 137-213; 289-413.

24. LUCHINS, A. S., & FORGUS, R. H. The effect of differential post weaning environment on the rigidity of an animal's behavior. J. genet. Psychol., 1955, 86, 51-58.

25. MELZACK, R. The genesis of emotional behavior: An experimental study of the dog. J. comp. physiol. Psychol., 1954, 47, 166-168.

26. MILNER, ESTHER A. A study of the relationships between reading readiness in grade one school children and patterns of parent-child interaction. Child Develpm., 1951, 22, 95-112.

27. PASAMANICK, B., KNOBLOCH, HILDA, & LILIENFELD, A. M. Socioeconomic status and some precursors of neuropsychiatric disorder. Amer. J. Orthopsychiat., 1956, 26, 594-601.

28. SCHWESINGER, GLADYS C. Heredity and environment. New York: Macmillan, 1933.

29. SCOTT, J. P., & CHARLES, MARGARET S. Some problems of heredity and social behavior. J. gen. Psychol., 1953, 48, 209-230.

30. SCOTT, J. P., & FULLER, J. L. Research on genetics and social behavior at the Roscoe B. Jackson Memorial Laboratory, 1946-1951 - A progress report. J. Hered., 1951, 42, 191-197.

31. SEARLE, L. V. The organization of hereditary maze-brightness and maze-dullness. Genet. Psychol. Monogr., 1949, 39, 279-325.

32. SNYDER, L. H. The genetic approach to human individuality. Sci. Man., N. Y., 1949, 68, 165-171.

33. SNYDER, L. H., & DAVID, P. R. The principles of heredity. (5th ed.) Boston: Heath, 1957.

34. SPOERL, DOROTHY T. Bilinguality and emotional adjustment. J. abnorm. soc. Psychol, 1943, 38, 37-57.

35. THOMPSON, W. R., & MELZACK, R. Early environment. Sci. Amer., 1956, 194 (1), 38-42.

36. THYON, R. C. Genetic differences in maze learning ability in rats. Yearb. mat. Soc. Stud. Educ., 1940, 39, Part I, 111-119.

37. WHITING, J. W. M., et al. Field guide for a study of socialization in five societies. Cambridge, Mass.: Harvard Univer., 1954 (mimeo.).

38. WHITING, J. W. M., & CHILD, I. L. Child training and personality: A cross-cultural study. New Haven: Yale Univer. Press, 1953.

39. WILLIAMS, JUDITH R., & SCOTT, R. B. Growth and development of Negro infants: IV. Motor development and its relationship to child rearing practices in two groups of Negro infants. Child Develpm., 1953, 24, 103-121.

40. WOODWORTH, R. S. Heredity and environment: A critical survey of recently published material on twins and foster children. Soc. Sci. Res. Coun. Bull., 1941, No. 47.

3. READ MORE PSYCHOLOGY CLASSICS

Superstition in the Pigeon

Burrhus Frederic "B. F." Skinner ranks among the most frequently cited and influential psychologists in the history of the discipline. Building on the behaviorist theories of Ivan Pavlov and John Watson he was the first psychologist to receive a Lifetime Achievement Award from the American Psychological Association (APA.) Originally published in 1948, Superstition in The Pigeon is a learning theory classic.

You can get hold of Superstition in The Pigeon via the following Amazon website link.

www.amazon.com/dp/B00DL6HL3Y

Transmission of Aggression Through Imitation of Aggressive Models: The Bobo Doll Experiment

Albert Bandura is one the world's most frequently cited psychologists. His ground-breaking work within the field of social learning and social cognitive theory led to a paradigm shift within psychology away from psychodynamic and behaviorist perspectives. As part of a new research agenda in the early 1960's which posited that people learn vicariously through observation Bandura began investigating aggression through imitation; work that gave rise to one of the most famous psychology studies of all time, "Transmission of Aggression Through Imitation of Aggressive Models." More commonly known as "The Bobo Doll Experiment," it was the first study to explore the impact of televised violence on children.

You can get hold of Transmission of Aggression Through Imitation of Aggressive Models: The Bobo Doll Experiment via the following Amazon website link.

www.amazon.com/dp/B00DHDC7Z8

Conditioned Emotional Reactions: The Case of Little Albert

Conditioned Emotional Reactions by John B. Watson and Rosalie Rayner is one of the most influential, infamous and iconic research articles ever published in the history of psychology. Commonly referred to as "The Case of Little Albert" this psychology classic attempted to show how fear could be induced in an infant through classical conditioning. Originally published in 1920, Conditioned Emotional Reactions remains among the most frequently cited journal articles in introductory psychology courses and textbooks.

One of the most dramatic aspects of Watson and Rayner's original study was that they had planned to test a number of methods by which they could remove Little Albert's conditioned fear responses. However, as Watson noted "Unfortunately Albert was taken from the hospital the day the above tests were made. Hence the opportunity of building up an experimental technique by means of which we could remove the conditioned emotional responses was denied us."

This unforeseen turn of events was something that obviously stayed with Watson, as under his guidance some three years later, Mary Cover Jones conducted a follow-up study - A Laboratory Study of Fear: The Case of Peter - which illustrated how fear may be removed under laboratory conditions. This additional and highly relevant article is also presented in full.

You can get hold of Conditioned Emotional Reactions: The Case of Little Albert via the following Amazon website link.

www.amazon.com/dp/B00BOVL3TQ

Significant Aspects of Client-Centered Therapy

Widely regarded as one of the most influential psychologists of all time, Carl Rogers was a towering figure within the humanistic movement towards person centered theory and non-directive psychotherapy.

Originally published in 1946 his classic article Significant Aspects of Client-Centered Therapy is essential reading for anybody interested in psychotherapy and counseling. In this landmark publication Carl Rogers outlines the origins of client-centered therapy, the process of client-centered therapy, the discovery and capacity of the client and the client-centered nature of the therapeutic relationship.

Significant Aspects of Client-Centered Therapy builds upon some of Carl Rogers' previously published work. Among the most notable of these earlier articles were The Processes of Therapy and The Development of Insight in A Counseling Relationship; both of which are also presented in full.

You can get hold of Significant Aspects of Client-Centered Therapy via the following Amazon website link.

www.amazon.com/dp/B00BSY6WGI

Hierarchy of Needs: A Theory of Human Motivation

A Theory of Human Motivation by Abraham H. Maslow is one of the most famous psychology articles ever written. Originally published in 1943, it was in this landmark paper that Maslow presented his first detailed representation of Self-Actualization - the desire to become everything that one is capable of becoming - at the pinnacle of a hierarchy of human needs.

In A Theory of Human Motivation Maslow draws upon some of his earlier published work. Three of these key references, Conflict, Frustration And The Theory of Threat, The Dynamics of Psychological Security-Insecurity and Preface To Motivation Theory are also presented in full.

You can get hold of Hierarchy of Needs: A Theory of Human

Motivation via the following Amazon website link.

www.amazon.com/dp/B004JKMUKU

4. CONNECT AND LEARN

Join thousands of psychology enthusiasts online.

Psychology on Facebook

www.facebook.com/psychologyonline

Psychology on Twitter

twitter.com/psych101

Psychology on Google+

goo.gl/hU8JL

Psychology on Linkedin

www.linkedin.com/groups/Psychology-Students-Network-4016322/about

Psychology on YouTube

www.youtube.com/user/LearnAboutPsychology

Psychology on Pinterest

pinterest.com/psychology

Psychology Student Guide

The Psychology Student Guide is designed for anyone who would like to learn more about what psychology actually is; anyone who is thinking about studying the subject or anyone who is currently a psychology student. See following Amazon website link for full details.

www.amazon.com/dp/B009ZC2UOS

The "ALL ABOUT" Website Portfolio

www.all-about-psychology.com

www.all-about-forensic-psychology.com

www.all-about-forensic-science.com

www.all-about-body-language.com

www.ingramcontent.com/pod-product-compliance
Lightning Source LLC
Chambersburg PA
CBHW070500290526
45790CB00003B/1030